Author:
Ian Graham earned a degree in applied physics at City University, London. He then earned a graduate degree in journalism. Since becoming a freelance author and journalist, he has written more than 250 children's nonfiction books.

Artists:
Caroline Romanet
Bryan Beach

Editor:
Jacqueline Ford

© The Salariya Book Company Ltd MMXVIII
No part of this publication may be reproduced in whole or in part, or stored in a retrieval system, or transmitted in any form or by any means, electronic, mechanical, photocopying, recording, or otherwise, without written permission of the publisher. For information regarding permission, write to the copyright holder.

Published in Great Britain in 2018 by
The Salariya Book Company Ltd
25 Marlborough Place, Brighton BN1 1UB

ISBN-13: 978-0-531-22769-5 (lib. bdg.) 978-0-531-23079-4 (pbk.)

All rights reserved.
Published in 2018 in the United States
by Franklin Watts
An imprint of Scholastic Inc.

A CIP catalog record for this book is available
from the Library of Congress.

Printed and bound in China.
Printed on paper from sustainable sources.
1 2 3 4 5 6 7 8 9 10 R 27 26 25 24 23 22 21 20 19 18

SCHOLASTIC, FRANKLIN WATTS, and associated logos are trademarks and/or registered trademarks of Scholastic Inc.

Scholastic Inc., 557 Broadway, New York, NY 10012

PAPER FROM
SUSTAINABLE
FORESTS

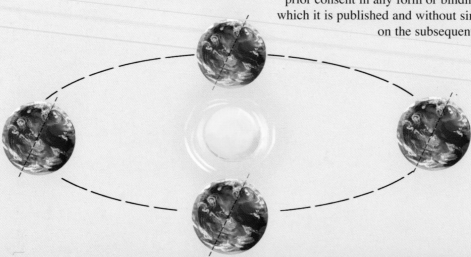

The Science of Weather

The Changing Truth About Earth's Climate

Written by
Ian Graham

Illustrated by
Caroline Romanet

Franklin Watts®
An Imprint of Scholastic Inc.

Contents

Introduction

Warm sunshine, bitterly cold wind, thunderstorms, snow, fog, thick clouds, rain, and a clear blue sky. They're all happening right now somewhere on Earth, and they're all types of weather. These day-to-day changes in nature affect our lives in all sorts of ways. We choose what to wear according to the weather. We might have to change our plans because a flood or snow has brought transportation to a halt. Farm crops thrive because of rain. Many of the towns and cities we live in are beside rivers and lakes that were created by rain. Wind-driven waves shaped our coastlines. Science can explain how and why all of these weather conditions happen.

The Atmosphere

Earth is surrounded by air. It's called the atmosphere. Most weather happens in the lowest part of the atmosphere closest to Earth's surface. This is called the troposphere. As you go higher, the air gets colder. That's why mountaintops are often covered with snow and ice.

Earth's atmosphere is about 300 miles (500 kilometers) thick and it has four main layers. From the ground upward, they're called the troposphere, stratosphere, mesosphere, and thermosphere.

Making Weather

Have you ever wondered why we have weather or where it comes from? The weather here on Earth is caused by the sun. Sunlight warms Earth's surface, which warms the air above it. The warm air rises. As it rises, it cools and sinks back toward the ground. But the warming is not the same everywhere. Land warms up faster than water, and clouds stop the sunshine from reaching some parts of the surface. Uneven warming and cooling, rising and falling, stirs up the air and produces the wind, clouds, rain, snow, and storms that we know as weather.

I wonder what the weather will be like today?

Highs and Lows

The atmosphere presses down on Earth's surface. This pressing is called air pressure. When air warms or cools, the pressure changes. Low pressure means clouds, rain, and storms. High pressure means clear skies and calm weather. Look at a weather map on TV or in a newspaper, and you'll see the high and low pressure areas.

Fascinating Fact

When air rises or falls, it doesn't go straight up or down. Earth's spinning motion makes it spiral. It spirals in different directions on opposite sides of the equator. This is called the Coriolis Effect.

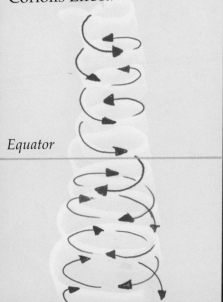

Equator

Rising and Falling

Changes in air pressure affect the weather because they make air float upward or sink downward. Low-pressure air rises higher where it is colder. Moisture in the air forms clouds. High-pressure air sinks lower where it is warmer. The clouds evaporate and so the air is clear.

Air pressure at Earth's surface is produced by the weight of the air. About 14.5 pounds of air presses on every square inch (or 1 kilogram of air presses on every square centimeter).

9

Inside a Cloud

The droplets of water that make up clouds are less than a thousandth of an inch (0.025 millimeters) across, or about five times thinner than a sheet of paper. They may be tiny, but there are so many of them that a cloud can hold thousands of tons of water.

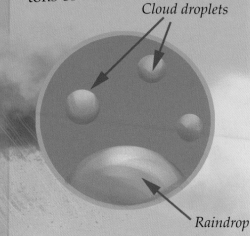

Cloud droplets

Raindrop

With only 800 hours of sunshine a year, the Prince Edward Islands in Antarctica are among the cloudiest places on Earth. The sunniest place—Yuma, Arizona—has 4,015 hours.

Clouds

C louds can be thin and hazy, white and fluffy, or big, dark, and scary, but they're all made of the same stuff—water. The water might be gassy moisture, liquid drops, or solid ice crystals. It comes from Earth's surface. Sunshine warms water on the surface and it evaporates (changes from a liquid to a gas). Rising air currents carry the moisture up into the sky and it cools down. As it cools, it forms tiny water droplets or ice crystals. These reflect sunlight in all directions, which is why clouds are often white.

Fog forms in the same way as clouds, but it's on the ground instead of high in the sky. If smoke mixes with fog, it's called smog.

Types of Clouds

There are three main types of clouds—stratus, cumulus, and cirrus. Stratus and cumulus are the lowest in the atmosphere. Stratus are flat, layered, spread-out clouds that often produce rain. Cumulus are fluffy clouds that can grow into storm clouds. The highest, cirrus, are wispy, feathery clouds made of ice crystals.

Stratus   *Cumulus*   *Cirrus*

Dusty Droplets

Moisture in cold air has to touch something solid, like specks of dust, before it will change into a cloud of water droplets. The trails you often see behind jet planes form in the same way. Specks of chemicals in burned fuel make moisture from the engines change first into water droplets and then into ice crystals.

Can You Believe It?

In dry places, clouds can be made to produce rain by firing tiny particles into them. This is called cloud seeding.

The particles are dropped from planes or fired from the ground. Raindrops form around the particles.

q

Monsoon Rains

Every summer, wet winds blow inland over the hot land of southwest India. The heat makes the air rise quickly and cool down, triggering heavy downpours. In winter, the winds change direction and blow out to sea. These seasonal winds are called monsoons.

Rain

Rain can be annoying when it ruins a day out. It can also be dangerous when it causes floods. But you'd better get used to it, because rain is vital for life. Creatures that live in the sea can survive in salty water, but land animals need freshwater. Rain provides it. Without rain, there would be very little freshwater on Earth, and life might never have developed on land. The next time you feel miserable because cold rain is running down your neck, remember that you wouldn't be here at all if rain didn't exist!

The air in the tropics is so warm that up to half of all the rain that falls evaporates before it hits the ground.

Rain, rain, go away!

The Water Cycle

Nature constantly recycles water. Rain is part of this worldwide circulation called the water cycle. The sun warms water, which evaporates and forms clouds. Rain and snow fall from the clouds to Earth's surface, where the sun warms them and the whole cycle begins once again.

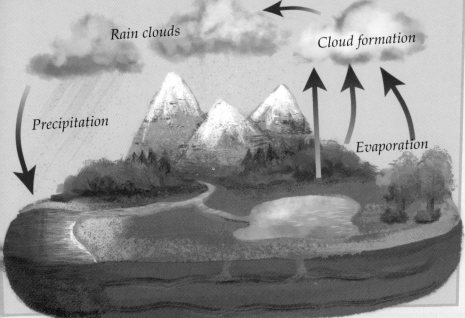

Rain clouds

Cloud formation

Precipitation

Evaporation

What Is a Rainbow?

Stand with your back to the sun when it peeks out on a rainy day and you might see a rainbow. It happens because sunlight shines into raindrops in the distance and bounces back out toward you. This spreads out the sunlight into lots of different colors, which you see as a rainbow.

Sunlight is not the only light that can make a rainbow. Moonlight can produce faint "moonbows," although these are very rare because moonlight is so dim.

Can You Believe It?

The water you drink today has been circulating on Earth for millions and millions of years. It might once have fallen as rain on a dinosaur. Isn't that an amazing thought?

Hot and Cold

It feels great to be outdoors on a sunny day, but the temperature doesn't have to rise or fall very much before the weather becomes uncomfortable or even dangerous. Heat is always on the move and it always flows from hot things to cold things. It flows from the sun to Earth, from the tropics to the poles, from hot land to cool air, and from warm sea to cold air. Eventually, it escapes into space and is replaced by more heat from the sun.

Chilly Poles

The weather is hot in the tropics and cold at the poles. This difference in temperature is caused by Earth's shape. In the tropics, the sun is overhead and sunlight is intense. Near the poles, Earth's curved surface spreads out sunlight over a bigger area, weakening its warming effect.

Sunlight

Equator

Hot weather is so cool!

Heat Wave

A heat wave is a spell of unusually hot weather that lasts for at least a few days. It happens when a giant bubble of high-pressure air settles over the land and stays there. Like a blanket, it traps hot air on the ground, day after day.

I hate heat waves!

Try It Yourself

Water expands (gets bigger) and contracts (gets smaller) when it changes temperature. You can see this for yourself by leaving a bottle of water in the freezer overnight. As the water turns to ice it gradually expands, making the bottle swell and crack. (See why on page 17.)

Heat makes most materials expand. On a hot day, the Eiffel Tower in Paris, France, is about 6 inches (15 cm) taller than on a cold day.

What Is a Mirage?

Heat can make you see things that aren't there! When the ground is hot, you might see a shimmering lake in the distance. It's really a piece of sky. Light from the sky is bent toward your eyes by hot air on the ground. This is called a mirage.

Why Does Earth Tilt?

Billions of years ago, a planet the size of Mars crashed into Earth. The two planets became one. The impact pushed Earth over so that it tilted at 23.5 degrees. Pieces of both planets were thrown into space. Gravity pulled them together and they formed the moon.

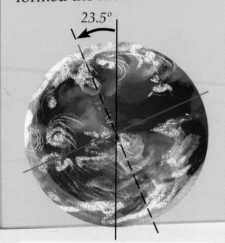

23.5°

Earth travels around the sun in 365.25 days, the length of a year. It also spins once every 24 hours, the length of a day and night.

The Seasons

As the months go by, the weather changes in a pattern that repeats itself every year. These periods of warm, cold, wet, and dry weather each year are the seasons. The four seasons—spring, summer, fall, and winter—are caused by the way Earth is tilted as it travels around the sun. Near the equator, the temperature changes very little during the year, but rainfall levels change a lot. Here, there are only two seasons—a wet season and a dry season.

Summer

Fall

Spring

Winter

The Four Seasons

When the northern half of Earth leans toward the sun, it's summer there, and winter in the southern half of Earth. Six months later, the northern half of Earth leans away from the sun—so then it's winter there, and summer in the southern half.

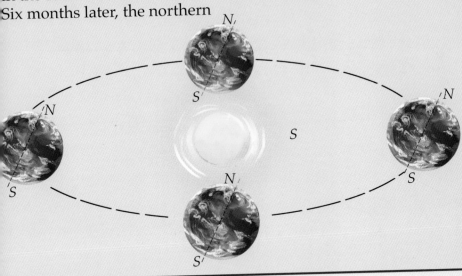

The names of the seasons come from ancient words. The word spring means "to rise." Summer means "half year." Autumn means "maturing" (growing older). Winter means "wet" or "water."

Midnight Sun

At the North Pole, Earth's tilt means that the sun doesn't dip below the horizon for six months. There is still daylight at midnight! At the South Pole, the sun doesn't rise for six months. Then it's the North Pole's turn to be dark while the South Pole has 24-hour sunshine.

It's midnight.

Fascinating Fact

Some reindeer live in darkness for weeks when the sun doesn't rise during winter in the far north. Their eyes change color, from gold in summer to blue in winter, to let them see better in the dark.

The most snowfall in any one-year period was 102 feet (31.5 meters) on Mount Rainier in Washington State, from February 19, 1971, to February 18, 1972.

Snow and Ice

If very cold rain falls on even colder surfaces, the rain freezes. It can cover trees, cars, or even whole buildings with a thick coating of ice. The ice can build up until it's heavy enough to bring down trees and power lines. If the temperature of the air inside a cloud falls below freezing, moisture in the cloud forms ice crystals instead of rain. As the tiny ice crystals blow around inside the cloud, more moisture freezes onto them, producing snowflakes.

Starry Flakes

Have you ever wondered why star-shaped snowflakes always have six points? It happens because of the shape of the water molecules that form them. The water molecules join together six at a time, forming a six-sided ring. Then the rings join together to make six-pointed snowflakes.

16

Frost in the Morning

If air on the ground cools down enough, moisture in the air forms water droplets. This is called dew, and it often appears after a cold night. If the ground is even colder, the moisture freezes and covers the ground with glistening, white frost.

It's frosty tonight.

Why It Happens

Water pipes sometimes burst in winter. It happens because of water's unusual behavior. Liquids usually shrink as they get colder. Water shrinks until it reaches 39°F (4°C), but then it starts expanding again as it freezes.

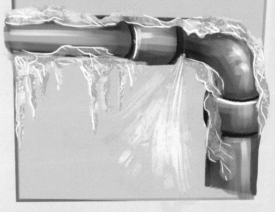

Snowflakes drift downward at a gentle 3 miles per hour (5 kilometers per hour), but large hailstones can hit the ground at more than 100 miles per hour (161 kph!)

What Is a Blizzard?

Heavy snow and strong winds can produce a severe snowstorm called a blizzard. Wind blows the snow into deep drifts. There can be so much snow blowing around in the air and covering the ground that everything looks white in all directions. This is called a whiteout.

Wish I'd gone to Jamaica!

17

Jet Streams

Strong winds called jet streams blow around the world high in the atmosphere. The fastest are the polar jet streams, near the North and South Poles. They can reach 250 miles per hour (400 kph) or more. The jet streams affect weather by moving storms around the planet like an express train.

Polar jet stream

Subtropical jet stream

The distant planet Neptune has the fastest winds in the solar system. Scientists have measured their top speed at an amazing 1,300 miles per hour (2,100 kph).

Blowing a Gale

Air rarely stands still anywhere for very long. The ever-changing pattern of high pressure and low pressure constantly pushes air around the planet. The moving air can make anything from a gentle breeze to a gale powerful enough to shatter buildings. Wind also whips up the sea's surface, producing the waves that break on our seashores. Wind helped to shape our history by powering the sailing ships that carried explorers, settlers, and traders across the oceans to new lands. Today, it powers the spinning blades of wind turbines that make electricity.

The Fastest Winds

A tornado is a funnel-shaped whirlpool of wind that sometimes comes spinning out of a thundercloud. Tornadoes produce the fastest winds on Earth, blowing at up to 318 miles per hour (512 kph). They behave like giant vacuum cleaners. The most powerful ones can even pick up a truck!

There are over a thousand tornadoes recorded every year in the United States. Many of these occur in a region in the Midwest known as Tornado Alley.

Trade Winds

Warm air in the tropics rises and moves toward the poles. Cooler air replaces it. North of the equator, these cool surface winds blow from the northeast. South of the equator, they blow from the southeast. We get the name "trade winds" from an old phrase, to "blow trade," which means to blow steadily in the same direction.

→ Westerlies ← Northeasterly trade winds ← Southeasterly trade winds

Try It Yourself

Make a tornado in a bottle. Pour water into a plastic bottle until it's three-quarters full. Add a drop of soap and a pinch of glitter. Screw the top on tightly. Shake the bottle and move it quickly with a circular motion. Can you see a mini-tornado swirling around inside?

Thunder and Lightning

Thunderstorms can produce huge hailstones. The biggest ever recorded measured 8 inches (20.3 cm) across. It fell in Vivian, South Dakota, on July 23, 2010.

Thunderclouds

The clouds that produce thunderstorms are called cumulonimbus. These towering clouds can reach a height of more than 12 miles (20 km). They are so high that they reach the top of the troposphere. There, the clouds spread out sideways, giving them a flat top and a nickname—anvil cloud.

The most extreme weather that many of us will experience is a thunderstorm. It's a violent storm with dazzling flashes of lightning and booming claps of thunder. It can also produce strong winds, heavy rain, and hailstones made of solid ice. Rain during thunderstorms can be heavy enough to cause flooding. These extreme storms usually last for less than an hour. They can happen anywhere, but they occur most often in the tropics, where hot air carrying lots of moisture from a warm ocean rises rapidly into ice-cold air higher up.

Inside a Thunderstorm

When hot, moist air rises, it cools and forms a cloud. A thundercloud continues rising and cools even more. Raindrops and ice crystals form and fall through the cloud. Strong rising air currents then blow them upward again. Eventually, they grow so big and heavy that they fall as intense rain or hailstones.

Anvil

Wind

Rain and hail

Lightning Flashes

As ice crystals travel up and down inside a thundercloud, they hit each other and become charged with electricity. Giant electric sparks fly between different parts of the cloud, and between the cloud and the ground. These sparks are lightning flashes that are hotter than the surface of the sun.

The scientific study of lightning is called fulminology. Scientists study lightning by flying aircraft through thunderstorms and firing rockets into thunderclouds to attract lightning.

Why It Happens

Buildings escape damage from lightning strikes by using a lightning rod or conductor. This is a metal rod or wire that leads the lightning all the way from the top of the building down to the ground.

Typhoon Tip

The worst tropical cyclone ever recorded was Typhoon Tip in 1979. It formed in the Pacific Ocean and was 1,380 miles (2,220 km) across. It would have covered the United States from Canada all the way to Mexico.

* Area the storm would have covered if it had crossed the United States.

Tropical cyclones occur in late summer, when the ocean is warmest. There are usually about six hurricanes every year in the Atlantic, but there can be up to 15.

Mega-Storms

Giant storms called tropical cyclones are the biggest, most powerful storms of all. They form in the moist air over warm oceans near the equator. Fed by ocean heat and moisture, they grow into huge rotating storms up to 500 miles (800 km) across. They travel across the ocean, growing more powerful until they reach a large landmass, which cuts off their supply of moisture, and then they quickly fade away. These monster storms are called hurricanes in the Atlantic, Caribbean, and Eastern Pacific; typhoons in the Western Pacific; and cyclones in the Indian Ocean and Australia.

In a Spin

Tropical cyclones always rotate (spin). When they form north of the equator, they spin in a counterclockwise direction. South of the equator, they spin in the opposite direction. They never cross the equator from one side to the other. Once they form, they always move away from the equator.

Tropical cyclones usually move across Earth's surface at a speed of 10 to 15 miles per hour (16 to 24 kph), although some can be more than twice as fast as this.

Making a Hurricane

Hurricanes form only where there is a very warm ocean. The water temperature must be at least 80°F (27°C). The water heats the air and it rises, forming a giant rotating spiral of rain clouds and thunderstorms. The center of the spiral, called the eye, is clear and calm.

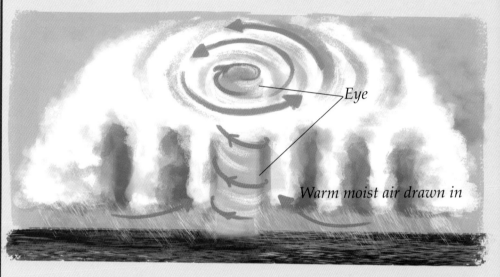

Eye

Warm moist air drawn in

Fascinating Fact

The fastest winds in a tropical cyclone blow around the circular eye in the middle, but the weather inside the eye itself is calm. The eye can be up to 40 miles (65 km) across.

Forecasting the Weather

P eople have been trying for thousands of years to predict, or forecast, the weather. They looked for weather patterns that might repeat in the future. They watched how their animals behaved before storms or fair weather. Today, thousands of weather stations all over the world provide millions of weather measurements every day. Weather balloons probe the atmosphere, and spacecraft photograph weather systems as they move around the planet. Supercomputers use this information to produce weather forecasts.

Buoys at Sea

Much of the weather that affects us on land develops far away over the oceans. Ships, planes, and floating buoys collect weather information from these remote places. The buoys are solar powered. Their instruments take weather measurements automatically and send them to weather centers by radio.

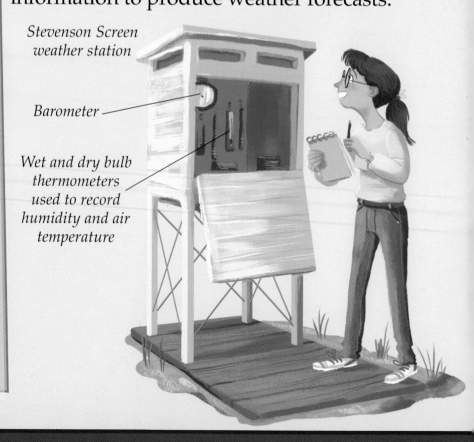

Stevenson Screen weather station

Barometer

Wet and dry bulb thermometers used to record humidity and air temperature

The first daily weather forecasts appeared in the London newspaper The Times in 1861. Weather forecasts on the radio began in Wisconsin in 1921. Television forecasts followed in the United Kingdom in 1936.

Number Crunching

The weather all over the world is so interconnected that predicting the weather in New York or London means forecasting the weather for the whole world. Only the world's fastest computers can do this. The supercomputers used by weather forecasters can do more than a trillion calculations per second.

Eyes in Space

Weather satellites in space watch Earth night and day. They take photographs showing the curls of clouds that mark areas of low pressure and storms. Forecasters can watch storms growing and track their movements. They can see dangerous storms approaching land, and warn people in danger to take cover.

Fascinating Fact

A weather satellite 22,300 miles (36,000 km) above the equator orbits Earth every 24 hours, the same time Earth takes to spin once. A satellite in this orbit stays above the same part of Earth.

25

The world wind speed record is 253 miles per hour (407 kph). It was set by a gust of wind during Tropical Cyclone Olivia at Barrow Island, Australia, in 1996.

Record Breakers

From time to time, the weather conditions in some places are perfect for producing record-breaking extremes. Temperatures might climb higher or fall lower than anywhere else on Earth. Rainfall might be heavier somewhere on one day than it has been since records began in the nineteenth century. Weather records since this time show that the world is gradually warming. This change will not only produce higher temperatures, but also longer droughts, stronger winds, and more violent storms—so today's records are very likely to be broken in the future.

Hottest

Furnace Creek in Death Valley, California, holds the record for the hottest place on Earth. On July 10, 1913, the air temperature there reached 134°F (56.7°C). The ground can be even hotter. On July 15, 1972, a ground temperature of 201°F (93.9°C) was recorded at Furnace Creek.

Ouch! Hot!

FURNACE CREEK

wettest

With annual rainfall of 39 feet (11.9 m), Mawsynram in northeast India is the wettest place on Earth. Most of the rain falls in only four months, between June and September. It's so wet that local farmers wear turtle-shaped rain shields made of bamboo and grass.

Coldest

In 1983, a bone-chilling record low temperature of -128.6°F (-89.2°C) was recorded at a scientific research base in Antarctica called Vostok Station. The coldest place on Earth where people live permanently is a Russian village called Oymyakon, where the temperature reached a record low of -89.9°F (-67.7°C) in 1933.

SOUTH POLE

The longest drought ever lasted for 173 months, or more than 14 years. It happened in Arica, Chile, where not one raindrop fell between 1903 and 1918.

Can You Believe It?

You can figure out the temperature by listening to a cricket. Crickets chirp faster in warm air. Adding 37 to the number of chirps in 15 seconds gives the temperature in degrees Fahrenheit!

CHIRP CHIRP CHIRP

Climate Change

Global warming has happened in the past, but not as fast as now. Earth is warming 10 times faster now than at any time in the past 65 million years.

A Warmer World

During this century, scientists think the world's temperature will rise by at least 0.5°F (0.3°C), and perhaps as much as 8.6°F (4.8°C). Gases like carbon dioxide that are causing this warming are called greenhouse gases. A warmer world is likely to have worse droughts that last longer.

Weather is what's happening in the atmosphere today and for the next few days. Climate is how the atmosphere behaves over a long time—decades, centuries, or even longer. Scientists have discovered that the climate is changing. The vast amounts of coal, oil, and natural gas that we have burned in the past 150 years have added more carbon dioxide to the atmosphere. An atmosphere with more carbon dioxide retains more heat from the sun, so it gradually warms up. A warming atmosphere will change our weather in the future.

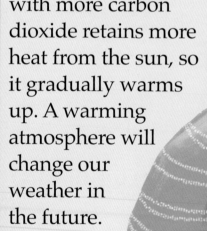

It's getting warmer and drier.

Warmer Water

With higher rainfall and more intense storms in some places, flooding is likely to become more common in the future. Meanwhile, warmer oceans fed by water from melting snow and ice, especially in the northern half of Earth, will lead to a rise in sea level. This is already happening.

A Stormy Future

Heat is a form of energy, so the atmosphere is a giant store of energy. Global warming will add more energy to the atmosphere, and some of it will probably make storms more intense and extreme. This means that future storms will probably produce faster winds and heavier rain.

So this is global warming …

The temperature of the whole Earth is higher now than it has been at any time in the past thousand years, and possibly a lot longer ago than that.

Fascinating Fact

If there were no greenhouse gases at all in Earth's atmosphere, our planet would be a lot colder. Without them, Earth's average temperature would be only 0°F (-18°C) instead of 59°F (15°C).

Without greenhouse gases, everywhere would be like this.

29

Glossary

Absolute zero The coldest possible temperature, -459.67°F (-273.15°C).

Air The mixture of gases that forms Earth's atmosphere.

Air pressure The pressing effect of the atmosphere, caused by the weight of the air being pulled down toward Earth's surface by gravity.

Atmosphere The layer, or layers, of gas that surround a planet. Earth's atmosphere is made of air.

Carbon dioxide A gas found in small amounts in Earth's atmosphere. Carbon dioxide traps heat, like a greenhouse, and so it is known as a greenhouse gas.

Climate The behavior of Earth's atmosphere over a long period of time.

Coriolis Effect The effect of Earth's spinning motion on moving objects, including air.

Cyclone A large mass of air rotating around a center of low atmospheric pressure anywhere in the world.

Drought A long period of time with very little rain, or none at all.

Equator An imaginary line around the middle of Earth that is equally distant from the North and South Poles.

Evaporate Change from a liquid to a vapor (gas).

Eye The circular region of calm, clear air at the center of a tropical cyclone.

Global warming The rise in temperature of Earth's atmosphere, caused by an increase in the amount of carbon dioxide and other greenhouse gases in the atmosphere.

Hurricane A tropical cyclone in the Atlantic Ocean, Caribbean Sea, or Eastern Pacific Ocean.

Jet stream A band of fast high-altitude wind blowing around the world, mainly from west to east.

Mesosphere A layer of Earth's atmosphere, above the stratosphere and below the thermosphere.

Mirage An optical illusion caused by a layer of hot air just above the ground.

Molecule A group of atoms joined together.

Monsoon A seasonal wind. Summer monsoons bring heavy rain to parts of South Asia and Southeast Asia. Winter monsoons are dry.

Satellite A moon or spacecraft that orbits a larger body, especially a planet.

Solar power Electric current made from sunlight.

Stratosphere The layer of Earth's atmosphere above the troposphere and below the mesosphere.

Thermosphere The highest layer of Earth's atmosphere, from the top of the mesosphere to the vacuum of outer space.

Tornado A funnel-shaped column of high-speed wind.

Trade wind A wind that blows steadily toward the equator from the northeast in the northern hemisphere and from the southeast in the southern hemisphere.

Tropical cyclone An intense rotating storm that forms over a warm ocean. Also known as a hurricane, typhoon, or cyclone in different parts of the world.

Troposphere The lowest layer of Earth's atmosphere, where most of the weather happens, from Earth's surface up to the next layer, the stratosphere.

Typhoon A tropical cyclone in the Western Pacific Ocean.

Water cycle The natural process that moves water from the land and oceans to the atmosphere and back to Earth's surface again.

Index

A
absolute zero 12
air pressure 7, 18
Antarctica 27
anvil cloud 20
atmosphere 6, 18, 28, 29

B
blizzard 17

C
climate change 28
cloud 5, 6, 7, 8, 16, 20
cloud seeding 9
Coriolis Effect 7
cyclone 22

D
dew 17
dinosaur 11
drought 27, 28

E
equator 7, 12, 14, 23

F
flood 5, 10, 20, 29
fog 5, 9
frost 17
fulminology 21

G
global warming 28, 29
greenhouse gas 28, 29

H
hailstone 17, 20
heat wave 13
hurricane 22, 23

I
ice 6, 8, 16, 21, 29

J
jet stream 18

L
lightning 20, 21

M
mesosphere 6
midnight sun 15
mirage 13
monsoon 10
moon 14
moonbow 11

N
Neptune 18

P
poles 12, 15, 18

R
rain 5, 6, 10, 11, 16, 23, 26, 27, 29
rainbow 11

S
satellite 24, 25
sea level rise 29
seasons 14, 15
smog 9
snow 5, 6, 11, 16, 17, 29
solar system 18
storm 6
stratosphere 6
sunshine 5, 6, 8, 11, 12
supercomputers 24, 25

T
temperature 12, 16, 23, 26, 27, 28, 29
thermosphere 6
thunderstorm 5, 18, 19, 23
Tornado Alley 19
tornado 19
trade winds 19
tropical cyclone 22, 23, 26
tropics 12
troposphere 6, 20
typhoon 22
Typhoon Tip 22

W
water cycle 11
waves 5, 18
weather forecasting 24, 25
whiteout 17
wind 6, 17, 18, 19, 20, 22, 23, 26, 29
wind turbine 18

32